Take a Closer Look at

Oil

by JoAnn Early Macken

RED
CHAIR
•PRESS•™

Please visit our website at **www.redchairpress.com** for more high-quality products for young readers.

About the Author: JoAnn Early Macken has written more than 130 books for young readers. JoAnn earned her M.F.A. in Writing for Children and Young Adults at Vermont College of Fine Arts. She has taught writing at four Wisconsin colleges, and she speaks about poetry and writing to children and adults at schools, libraries, and conferences.

Publisher's Cataloging-In-Publication Data
Macken, JoAnn Early, 1953-
     Take a Closer Look at Oil / by JoAnn Early Macken. -- [First edition].

     pages : illustrations, maps, charts ; cm

Summary: Oil and gas make up nearly half of all the energy we use, but these fuels are being used up. What alternatives do we have in a future with limited oil and fossil fuels? Learn how scientists are looking for new ways to produce and replace these fossil fuels. STEM career opportunities are featured. Includes a glossary and references for additional reading.
   "Core content library"--Cover.
   Interest age level: 006-010.
   Edition statement supplied by publisher.
   Issued also as an ebook. (ISBN: 978-1-63440-059-6)
   Includes bibliographical references and index.
   ISBN: 978-1-63440-051-0 (library hardcover)

   1. Fossil fuels--Social aspects--Juvenile literature. 2. Renewable energy sources--Juvenile literature. 3. Fossil fuels. 4. Renewable energy sources. I. Title. II. Title: Take a closer look at oil III. Title: Oil

TP318.3 .M33 2016

333.8/2   2015937988

Illustration credits: Joe LeMonnier: 10, 17

Photo credits: Department of Energy: 11;   Shutterstock: cover, 1, 3, 4, 5, 6, 7, 8, 9, 11(top), 12, 13, 14, 15, 16, 17, 18, 19, 20, 21, 22, 23, 24, 25, 26, 27, 28, 29, 30, 31, 32, 33, 34, 35, 36, 37, 38, 39, 40

This series first published by:
Red Chair Press LLC   PO Box 333   South Egremont, MA 01258-0333

Printed in the United States of America
Distributed in the U.S. by Lerner Publisher Services. www.lernerbooks.com

112015 1P LPSS16

Contents

Chapter 1. How Did We Get to This Point? 4

Chapter 2. What's the Problem? 12

Chapter 3. What Can We Do to Help? 20

Chapter 4. Where Do We Go From Here? 28

STEM Career Connections 36

Resources 38

Glossary 39

Index 40

1 How Did We Get to This Point?

Visitors to the La Brea Tar Pits in Los Angeles, CA, can see a replica of a mammoth stuck in a tar pit.

Oil collects underground.

Millions of years ago, tiny animals and plants lived in Earth's oceans. They died there, too. Their bodies sank into mud. Over time, sand and silt piled up on them. Those heavy layers created heat and pressure, which turned the remains into **crude oil**, or **petroleum**. Oil, coal, and natural gas all form from ancient creatures. They are called **fossil fuels**.

Oil collects underground. Some of it leaks up through cracks called **seeps**. The oil is mixed with tar, natural gas, and water. Long ago, people dug up seeps to find oil.

Native Americans used oil from seeps as paint. They used tar to glue tools. They waterproofed baskets and canoes. Later settlers used oil in lamps, to grease machinery, and to pave roads.

Warm tar, or **asphalt**, is sticky. Animals can be trapped in it. The La Brea Tar Pits near Los Angeles, CA, is a famous seep. Visitors can see fossils from extinct animals.

Finding and Removing Oil

Now **geologists** search for oil. They study rocks and land features. They check satellite images. They use sound waves to map rock layers. Before they drill, oil companies study the impact on the environment. Workers build roads, clear trees, and level the land.

Tall **derricks** on land or on oil platforms at sea hold up drilling machinery. Underground, drill bits on long pipes cut through rock. Fluid pumped down through the pipes helps cool the machinery. It carries rock bits back up. A drill can reach down a mile or more to find oil.

★ Oil workers use sharp drill bits and many pipes to reach oil underground.

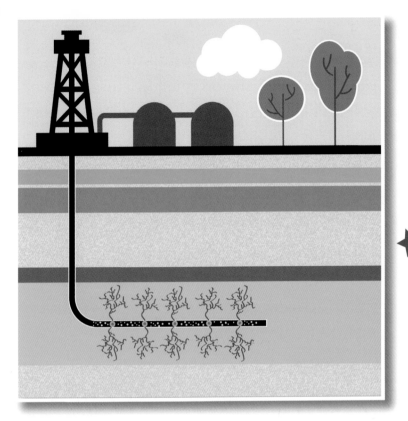

Hydraulic fracturing, or fracking, reaches oil and gas in rock.

Hydraulic fracturing, or **fracking**, reaches oil trapped in rock. Fluid is pumped in under high pressure. The fluid can contain water, chemicals, and sand. It dissolves channels in the rock. Oil and gas flow out. Geologists have not determined all the risks in fracking.

To reach oil underwater, companies drill offshore. Equipment rests on the seafloor, floats on a barge, or works from a ship or pontoon.

Companies make huge investments before they know whether a well will ever produce oil.

Oil Refining

Crude oil is dark, sticky, and not very useful. **Refining** turns it into other products. First, the oil must be transported to refineries. Tankers carry crude oil across oceans. Trains carry carloads over land. Crude oil flows through miles and miles of pipelines. Most pipes are buried underground. Some are underwater. Huge pumps force the oil through. Workers watch it move on computers.

At a refinery, crude oil is heated. It is pumped into a tall tower. Under pressure, it **evaporates**. Vapor rises. As it cools, it divides. Lighter liquids collect in trays near the top of the tower. Heavier ones drop to the bottom.

These liquids can be broken down to make new products. They can be combined with other ingredients.

In a refinery, these and other products are made from crude oil:

- gasoline
- diesel fuel
- heating oil
- liquid petroleum gas
- jet fuel
- asphalt

⭐ This oil tanker is small compared to most but it can still carry 120,000 metric tonnes of crude oil.

Bridge

Fuel tank

Empty

Engine room   Pump   Oil Tanks   Double hull
               room

Oil Use

Petroleum products fuel our vehicles. They heat our homes. They produce electric power.

The United States is now the largest oil producer in the world. It is also the largest oil user. The U.S. does not produce enough to meet all its needs. So it imports oil from other countries. The top sources are Canada, Saudi Arabia, Mexico, Venezuela and Nigeria.

Sources of U.S. petroleum imports

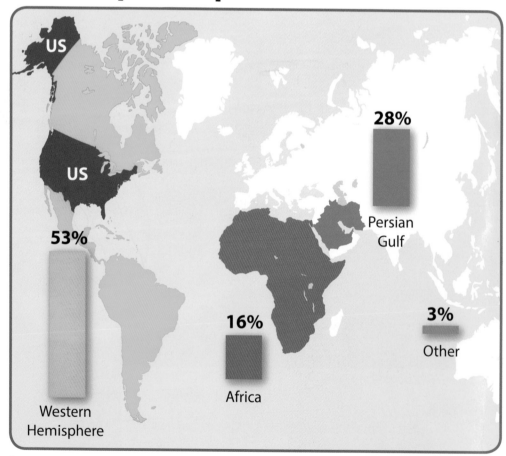

Source: U.S. Energy Information Administration, (2013 data; latest available)

Oil Reserves

The United States keeps an emergency supply of crude oil. It is stored in underground caverns along the Gulf Coast. The Strategic Petroleum Reserve can hold up to 727 million barrels. Home heating oil and gasoline are also stockpiled for Northeast U.S. residents.

 Aerial view of crude oil storage tanks near Nederland, TX.

These and other goods are made from petroleum products:

- tires
- medicine
- paint
- nylon
- plastic
- ink
- crayons
- dishwashing liquids
- CDs and DVDs

2 What's the Problem?

Oil is a nonrenewable resource. When it runs out, there is no more. As the supply shrinks, it becomes harder to reach. It also becomes more expensive. No one knows how long the oil that remains will last.

Burning petroleum products gives off gases. Carbon dioxide is the main **greenhouse gas**. It traps the sun's heat, which warms the planet. Other **toxic emissions** cause cancer and other serious health problems. Workers face health risks.

Water left over from fracking and drilling is injected into the ground. Oil removal has increased. The number of earthquakes in some areas has risen, too. Scientists are studying the connection.

Finding oil is no guarantee of prosperity. In Nigeria, for example, oil pollutes land, air, and water. Oil companies profit. So does the government. Many people still live in poverty.

⭐ Dolphins communicate with sound waves, called echolocation.

To search for oil offshore, workers create sound waves with air gun blasts. These sound waves could affect marine animals. Whales and dolphins communicate with sound. Scientists think their migration or feeding patterns could be disrupted. Fish might be scared away by noise.

Oil Spills

Some oil flows into waterways from natural seeps. But humans can cause bigger problems. Oil runs into rivers and lakes. It leaks from boats and jet skis. It spills from tanker ships. These spills can harm or kill people and wildlife. They can ruin fragile habitats.

Floating booms contain some spills on the water's surface. Workers on boats can scoop up the oil. Large sponges absorb some oil. Some oil spills are set on fire. Chemicals can break up oil slicks. But they are toxic to animals and people.

Oily birds and animals cannot stay warm. They lose water resistance. They swallow poison chemicals. Even cleanup workers can become ill from breathing spilled oil.

 A 2013 oil spill damaged beaches in Thailand.

Moving Oil through Pipelines

Workers patrol pipelines. They track oil flow on computers. But oil can leak before anyone spots it. Repairing a leak takes time. In the meantime, oil keeps spilling.

A pipeline can block an animal migration route. An Alaska pipeline is raised ten feet in some areas. This lets caribou walk beneath it. Other sections are buried. Animals can cross on top. An earthquake broke some supports, but the pipeline did not leak.

North American Pipeline Plans

More oil pipelines are being planned and built. Keystone XL would run more than one thousand miles from Alberta to the U.S. Gulf coast. It would extend the existing Keystone pipeline. The new XL line would transport up to 830,000 barrels of oil per day from the oil-rich areas of Alberta, Montana, and North Dakota. People who oppose pipelines worry about wildlife and oil spills. Supporters say using the pipelines is a cleaner and safer way to move oil than using trucks or trains through towns. Others say building pipelines creates jobs. But many jobs last only until pipelines are built.

Keystone Pipeline Route

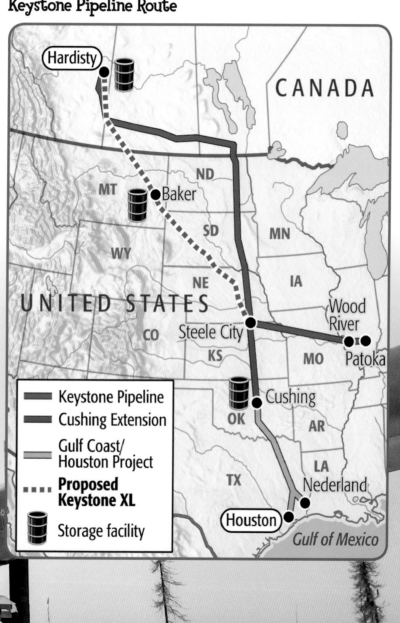

CANADA

Hardisty

ND

MT ● Baker

SD

WY

MN

IA

UNITED STATES

NE

CO

Steele City

KS

MO

Wood River

Patoka

Cushing

OK

AR

LA
Nederland

TX

Houston

Gulf of Mexico

Legend:
- Keystone Pipeline
- Cushing Extension
- Gulf Coast/ Houston Project
- **Proposed Keystone XL**
- Storage facility

Moving Oil by Rail

U.S. oil production is rising. Pipelines cannot keep up with the increased shipping. Almost a million barrels of crude oil move by train each day. Less room is left for other shipments. Farmers lose money while they wait to ship their crops. Passenger trains are held up for hours waiting for freight trains that run on the same tracks

Much of the oil travels through cities and towns. Old, unsafe tank cars are still in service. Railroads must tell emergency responders and rail yards about some large shipments. But they do not make the schedules or details public. If a train derails, tank cars can spill. The oil can catch fire.

In a horrific accident in Quebec, a 72-car train derailed. 1.6 million gallons of oil spilled. A huge fire broke out. 47 people were killed. In North Dakota, toxic smoke poured from a derailed train. A whole town had to be evacuated.

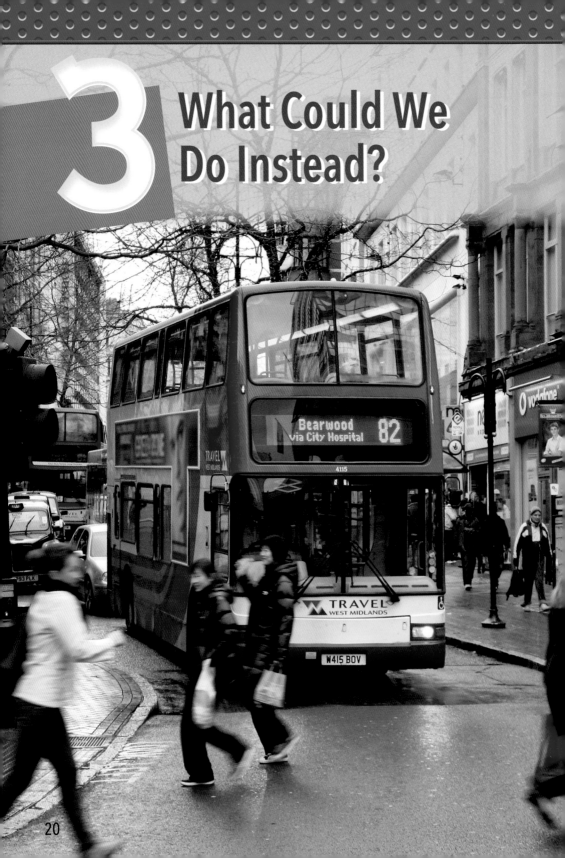

3 What Could We Do Instead?

Change our habits.

Transportation uses a lot of fossil fuel! Many people are used to taking cars, even on short trips. If we must keep driving, we could drive more wisely. Huge gas guzzlers waste fuel and pollute more than smaller cars. A hybrid car has a small gasoline engine. It also has an electric motor. They operate together, produce little pollution, and get good mileage.

The fewer cars on the road, the less pollution. Sharing rides can cut down the number of cars. Some cities encourage carpooling. They help set up groups. They set aside special lanes for carpoolers.

Where it's available, public transportation is a sound option. Making it available for more people would help us all change our habits. And walking is good for our health!

Many scientists and engineers are looking for new ways to produce energy in place of oil.

Biomass

Biomass is mostly plant matter that can produce energy. Burning wood to heat a home is a good example. Bamboo and other grasses are grown for fuel. So are some types of small trees. Plant parts like corn husks left in farm fields are used as biomass. Sawdust, branches, and leaves from processed trees are biomass. So are paper, yard waste, and animal waste. Many products made from fossil fuels can be made from biomass instead.

Hydroelectric Power

Water is a **renewable** energy source. It is the one used most in the United States. Running water spins turbines that run generators. Hydropower is the cheapest way to generate electricity.

Types of Energy We Use Today

- Gas 30%
- Coal 28%
- Oil* 19%
- Renewable 12%
- Nuclear 11%

Source: U.S. Energy
Information Administration

Hydropower plants are reliable. They are efficient. They produce less pollution than power plants that use fossil fuels. But construction is expensive. Dams can block wildlife routes. A dam failure could be catastrophic. Scientists are working to develop smaller projects. They can add up to more efficient electricity production.

Solar Power

Solar cells convert energy from the sun into electricity. Solar power plants provide clean energy. They are expected to provide more of the country's energy needs in the future.

Sunlight is free, but the technology to produce energy is expensive. As prices drop, consumer use rises. Homes, schools, and businesses are all turning to solar power. The total amount of energy solar provides is still small.

Wind Power

Wind spins the blade of a turbine. The motion turns a shaft that leads to a generator. Higher up, the wind is stronger. Higher wind speeds can create more power. Most wind turbines are mounted on towers. They can be connected to a power grid. Or they can run separately. Huge wind farms catch the power in open spaces.

Wind speeds vary, so the power supply is not steady. Wind turbines do not create pollution. But they do make noise. And bats and birds can fly into them.

Geothermal Power

Geothermal power uses heat from deep inside Earth. Wells are drilled into pools of hot water. The water can be piped through a building to warm it.

Steam from a hot pool can turn turbines. That creates electricity.

Fluid can be injected into hot pools. The fluid fractures rock. Hot water can flow up into pipes. The flowing water generates electricity. After it cools, the water is pumped back underground.

Wairakei geothermal power station, New Zealand

Nuclear Power

In nuclear power plants, radioactive uranium heats water. The water turns into steam. The steam turns a turbine. That creates electricity. But radiation is deadly. So reactors are lined with concrete and steel. Water cools the radioactive materials.

Nuclear power plants emit little greenhouse gas. But uranium is not renewable. It can take thousands of years to decay to safe levels. It corrodes containers. Cooling and storing it are expensive. Nuclear power accidents can kill huge numbers of people. They can destroy the environment.

4 Where Do We Go From Here?

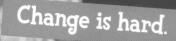

Change is hard.

The world's energy needs keep going up. We all want to better our lives. We all want our families to be warm and safe. We all want to be productive. Each generation wants to move forward.

How can we safely meet growing energy needs? How can we share energy fairly? Developed countries have caused most of the world's pollution. Developing nations want to do better, too.

Some people believe all fossil fuels should stay in the ground. Other energy sources cause less damage to the planet and its residents. Other people refuse to see what science has proven: Climate change is real. And using fossil fuels makes it worse.

U.S. petroleum use is expected to stay about the same through 2040. After that, who knows? Change is hard. People all over the world are moving toward better energy sources. They are looking for solutions to energy problems.

Clean Energy is Green Energy

Oil companies keep looking for ways to improve. New computer systems help them find oil more easily. They can drill fewer wells to explore. And each well can reach a larger area. Robotic oil rigs could drill faster than ever. They could keep workers safer. Communication keeps getting better. When oil does spill, companies can reach workers faster.

★ Inspectors on offshore oil rigs make sure everything is safe for the workers.

Governments can help. They can give tax breaks to clean energy users. The United States and China emit nearly half of the world's greenhouse gases. The two countries have agreed to new limits. And the U. S. government has pledged to cut its own emissions.

Scientists are working on ways to generate power from moving water. The tide turns an underwater turbine off the Maine coast. River currents can turn turbines, too. They can be placed so that animals can go around them. Smaller turbines could fit inside a city's water pipes. Someday, power could even be generated inside faucets.

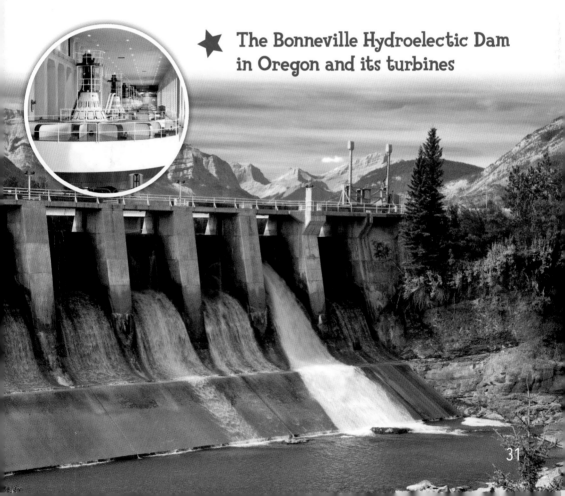

The Bonneville Hydroelectic Dam in Oregon and its turbines

New Sources of Power

On sunny summer days, solar energy produces power. Around the world, its use is growing. India and China are building new solar plants. So are Canada and Mexico. In France, some new buildings must include solar panels or green plants on their roof. Saudi Arabia is building a solar-powered plant to remove salt from drinking water. In Japan, solar panels float in water like islands.

Wind power use is up, too. Builders are looking for ways to include wind turbines in bridges and other structures.

★ Solar panels can be placed anywhere the sun is plentiful.

Scientists are finding ways to make substitutes for oil. Chemicals that now come from oil might one day be made from sugar. To avoid reducing the food supply, scientists plan to use wood rather than food plants to produce the sugar.

Harvard scientists have created a system they call a "bionic leaf." It changes solar energy into a liquid fuel.

 Solar panels line the Bhumibol Bridge in Thailand.

What Would We Do Without Oil?

Oil has fueled huge advances in the world. But it will not last forever. Lucky for us, we have other energy options. Wind, water, and sunlight are all free. Building the systems that use them can be expensive. But using them to generate power makes sense.

Some good news arrived in 2014. The world's economy grew 3 percent. But greenhouse gas emissions stayed the same as the year before. The 2013 level was the highest ever. So Earth is still in great danger. Emissions must fall to avoid more drastic warming. But in the past, any drop has always been linked to bad economic news. This time, it appears to be due to efforts to fight climate change.

★ Driving a hybrid or electric car can help reduce greenhouse gas emissions.

Scientists' hard work is starting to make a difference! We can all do something to help fight climate change. Using renewable energy is a smart way to start.

STEM Career Connections

All over the world, workers are needed in four key areas:

- Science
- Technology
- Engineering
- Math

Scientists work in research labs. They also go out in the world to observe. They collect data to study.

Technology puts science to practical use. Many STEM jobs are related to computers.

Engineers solve problems. They invent and design new products.

Math is a key skill in many kinds of jobs.

Energy industries keep growing. They will need trained workers for some time to come. They'll use math to figure out costs. They'll study science data. Think up new theories. Explore safer methods. Document methods. They might focus on these and other issues:

- replacements for petroleum products
- protecting the environment
- lowering costs of renewable energy

STEM skills help people working with energy in these fields:

- biomass and biofuels
- geothermal power
- heating and cooling
- hydropower
- nuclear power
- solar power
- transportation
- wind power

How will energy fit into your future?

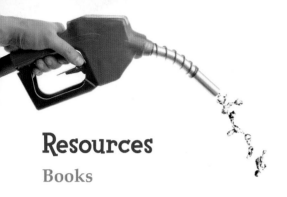

Resources

Books

Clean Energy by Laurie Goldman. Flash Point (2010)

Oil by John Farndon. DK Publishing (2012)

Oil Spill!: Disaster in the Gulf of Mexico by Elaine Landau. Millbrook Press (2011)

Sea Otter Rescue by Roland Smith. Puffin Books (1999)

Sun Power: A Book about Renewable Energy by Esther Porter. Capstone Press (2013)

Web Sites and Videos

Oil Spill in the Gulf of Mexico:
http://www.scholastic.com/browse/collection.jsp?id=745

Page Museum at the La Brea Tar Pits: http://www.tarpits.org/

The Story of Oil and Natural Gas video from the American Petroleum Institute: http://www.api.org/story/index.html

U.S. Energy Information Administration's **Energy Kids** site:
http://www.eia.gov/kids/index.cfm

U.S. Energy Mapping System:
http://www.eia.gov/state/maps.cfm?src=home-f3

Glossary

asphalt: tar, which forms when crude oil dries and thickens

crude oil: natural, unprocessed fossil fuel, that has been recovered from Earth.

derrick: a support for oil drilling machinery

emission: something emitted, or given off

evaporate: to change from a liquid into a gas

fossil fuel: oil, coal, and natural gas, which formed over time from heat and pressure on the remains of living creatures

fracking: hydraulic fracturing, a method of crushing rock to allow trapped oil to flow freely out

geologist: a person who studies Earth processes, materials, and history

greenhouse gas: a gas that traps and holds heat in the atmosphere. The main greenhouse gases are carbon dioxide, methane, nitrous oxide, and fluorinated gases

petroleum: crude oil and any products made by refining crude oil

refining: turning crude oil into more useful products

renewable: able to be replaced by nature

seep: a place where oil leaks up from Earth

toxic: poisonous

Index

biomass, *12*

careers, *19*

climate change, *7, 15*

derricks, *4*

drilling, *4, 7*

earthquake, *9*

earthquakes, *7*

fossil fuels, *3, 15*

fracking, *4, 7*

geologists, *4*

geothermal power, *14*

goods made from petroleum, *6*

governments, *16*

greenhouse gases, *7, 18*

health risks, *7*

hybrid cars, *11*

hydroelectric power, *12, 16*

importing oil, *6*

La Brea Tar Pits, *3*

marine animals, *8*

migration routes, *9*

Native Americans, *3*

natural gas, *3*

nuclear power, *14*

offshore drilling, *4*

oil reserves, *6*

oil spills, *8*

oil substitutes, *17*

petroleum products, *5*

pipelines, *5, 9*

poverty, *7*

prosperity, *7*

radiation, *14*

railroads, *10*

refining, *5*

reserves, *oil, 6*

seeps, *3, 8*

solar power, *13, 17*

sound waves, *4, 8*

STEM, *19*

tar, *3*

toxic emissions, *7*

train, *10*

transportation, *11*

transporting oil, *5*

turbines, *13*

uranium, *14*

wind power, *13, 17*